Table of Contents

ACKNOWLEDGMENTS

I would like to thank the following people for their help and advice with this book: Shari Nelson and Danny Scordato. And a special thanks to Ariadna Hernandez, an ESL student, for sacrificing her time and energy to try out the exercises and make suggestions to help me complete this book so that other English learners would be able to understand it. And to Dr. Jeanne Gilleland and Harry W. Rye for graciously editing this book.

Introduction

Americans love to use idioms, also called expressions. Because they are used so often, they are a faster way to understand American conversation. These expressions are heard constantly in movies, television shows, news, and, of course, daily conversation. The more idioms you know and use, the better your conversations and understanding of Americans will be. For example, you could say, "I worked hard today," and the listener would understand you. Or, to make your words more interesting, you could say the popular idiom, "**I worked like a dog**," and an American listener would immediately see the image in their mind and understand.

Research has shown that people remember words better when they are combined with images. One of the main benefits of this book is that pictures are provided for each idiom. In addition, this book helps you remember the expressions with lots of practice exercises and games. Games are fun and relaxing. The more relaxed you are while learning, the better you will remember information.

The reason that I wrote this book is because I found when I taught idioms in my ESL classes, the students remembered them much better with pictures. When I tried to find books that had idioms with pictures, there were only a few. And those books did not have pictures, exercises, and games combined to reinforce the material.

My hope for you is that you enjoy this book and have fun using the idioms. They are a great supplement to your English language training, and you will be speaking like an American **in no time** (quickly)!

Lesson 1 – Animal Idioms

Dialogue

Steve: Did I tell you that my cousins are coming over to our house?
Jennifer: No. Are you looking forward to seeing them?

Steve: Yes, but they think of us as the **black sheep** of the family because we aren't as rich as they are.
Jennifer: You could probably be rich too if you **worked like a dog,** but who wants to do that? You would just get stressed and have no time for fun.

Steve: I know. And, I have never been a **copycat**. I work hard, but I don't want to be like my cousins. Hey, I baked a pie for my cousins, and I have an extra one. Do you want to try a piece? It's delicious.
Jennifer: No thanks. I just quit eating sugar last week. I went **cold turkey**.

Steve: Don't be **pigheaded**. You know you want some pie. **Jennifer**: I'm not being stubborn. I appreciate the offer, but thanks anyway.

Steve: Oh, well. I guess I'll save it for my midnight snack since you are being a **chicken**.
Jennifer: Very funny. That's right. I forgot you are a **night owl**.
This **early bird** needs to go home and get to bed, so I can get up at 6:00 a.m.

Definitions:

(note: Ex. means example)

1. **(the) black sheep** – A person who embarrasses a family or another group because the person is different or has gotten into trouble. Ex. He is the black sheep of the family. He doesn't like working.

2. **(to) work like a dog** – A person who works very hard. Ex. He works like a dog.

3. **(a) copycat** – A person who copies another person's clothes, ideas, or behavior. Ex. She is a copycat. She wears the same clothes as me.

4. **(a) chicken** – A person who is afraid of something or someone. Ex. Don't be a chicken. Rollercoasters are fun.

5. **pigheaded** – A person who is stubborn, unwilling to change. Ex. My husband is so pigheaded. He will not dance with me.

6. **(to go) cold turkey**- to quit something completely. Ex. When I quit smoking, I went cold turkey. I'm not buying any more cigarettes.

7. **(a) night owl** – A person who likes to stay up very late. Ex. I am a night owl. I stay up till 3:00 a.m. every night.

8. **(an) early bird** – A person who gets up early or arrives to places early. Ex. My son is an early bird. He always gets up at around 6:00 a.m.

(the) black sheep	(a) chicken	(a) night o
(to) work like a dog	pigheaded	(an) early bi
(a) copycat	(to go) cold turkey	

Guess the meaning from the words in the box.

1. _____to be stubborn.

2. _____to work very hard.

3. _____the odd or different ones in the family.

4. _____someone who copies another person.

5. _____someone who is scared of someone or something.

6. _____to quit something completely.

7. _____to get up early or arrive early.

8. _____to stay up late.

Find and correct the one error in each idiom.

1. Don't be a chick. This is no monster in the closet.

2. He has always been a stubborn, bigheaded boy.

3. My mother quit smoking hot turkey.

4. They are the blank sheep of the family.

5. My father works like the dog. He's never home.

6. Ken is a night animal. He always stays up late.

7. My little sister is a coolcat. She always tries to dress like me.

8. Sheila is early again! She is such an early girl.

cold turkey

black sheep

night owl

chicken

pigheaded

early bird

work like a dog

copycat

Lesson 2 – Body Idioms

Dialogue

Sally: Do you remember my **nosy** neighbor Rose? Well, I asked her not to tell anyone about my car accident, but she has such **a big mouth**. My other neighbor, Ellen, said that Rose told her all about my car accident.

Diana: It's hard to trust people sometimes. I'm lucky that I **see eye to eye** with most of my neighbors. But one of them, Mike, is **a pain in the neck**. He always seems to come over to chat when I am talking on the phone or getting ready to go out.

Sally: We have a new neighbor whose name is Tom. I'm going to bring him a basket of fruit to welcome him to the neighborhood. I just hope I am not tempted to eat it first because of my **sweet tooth**.

Diana: Well, **on the one hand**, you can get to know your neighbor and see if he's single! But, **on the other hand**, what if he is diabetic and can't eat sugar?

Sally: Well, I'll **play it by ear**. If I see him outside, I'll say hello and try to find out what he's like.

Definitions:

1. **nosy**-wanting to know about other people's lives. Ex. My neighbor is very nosy. I always see her looking into the neighbors' windows.

2. **(a) big mouth**-A person who talks too much, especially about things that should be private. Ex. She has a big mouth. I told her not to tell my secret, but she did.

3. **(to) see eye to eye**-to agree with someone. Ex. My boyfriend and I see eye to eye on everything. We never fight about anything.

4. **(a) pain in the neck**-A person who is difficult or annoying. Ex. My boss is a pain in the neck. He always makes me work late.

5. **(to have a) sweet tooth**-to like sweets. My little girl has a sweet tooth. She loves anything with chocolate.

6. **on the one hand**-from one point of view. Ex. On the one hand, sugar tastes great.

7. **on the other hand**-from the opposite point of view. Ex. On the other hand, sugar can cause dental problems.

8. **(to) play it by ear**-to do something without planning. Ex. I don't know if I want to go to the festival yet. Let's play it by ear and see how the weather is.

nosy   (a) big mouth   (to) see eye to e`

(a) pain in the neck   (to have a) sweet tooth   (to) play it by e

on the one hand   on the other hand

Guess the meaning from the words in the box.

1. _____not planning ahead.

2. _____however

3. _____to be annoying

4. _____to agree

5. _____extremely curious about others

6. _____to like to gossip

7. _____one thing to consider is

8. _____to like sweets

Find and correct the one error in each idiom.

1. Sara is a nose person. She always checks to see if I am home.

2. Tom is a pain in the back. He always wants to borrow money from me.

3. On my one hand, I like her.

4. On the other hands, I don't know if I trust her.

5. We can play them by ear. I'll let you know later if I can go.

6. I just love chocolate. I have such a sweet teeth.

7. My little sister, Emily, has a large mouth. She cannot keep a secret.

8. Do they see eye two eye?

nosy

big mouth

see eye to eye

pain in the neck

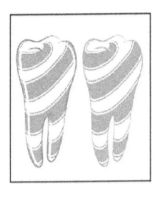

sweet tooth

on the one hand

on the other hand

play it by ear

Games for Reviewing

Word Search for Chapters 1 & 2

Read the clues below (1-16) and find the missing part of the idiom or the meaning.

```
B  H  F  B  A  S  T  N  Z  D  B  E  R  B  L  E
C  I  J  T  C  M  A  X  W  J  R  D  N  K  W  Y
X  Y  G  T  O  B  H  A  H  N  E  C  K  K  K  W
T  S  A  A  L  W  H  T  X  K  V  H  C  F  E  E
B  H  E  U  D  N  O  S  Y  Q  E  A  R  L  Y  L
G  I  V  E  F  J  J  K  V  I  B  P  A  L  Q  C
U  C  O  P  Y  Y  V  H  X  J  T  O  O  T  H  P
F  U  H  E  A  D  E  D  D  K  U  F  A  S  L  O
D  B  W  X  F  E  A  R  G  D  J  T  V  E  X  W
L  O  K  C  K  R  F  M  W  V  A  G  X  D  X  L
A  K  G  X  V  C  H  I  C  K  E  N  O  L  N  C
V  O  L  O  E  B  K  Q  B  Z  U  M  B  N  C  M
B  G  C  T  Z  W  K  K  K  L  C  W  V  V  E  F
Q  A  B  H  R  S  Y  O  I  F  A  K  A  N  Y  R
U  D  Q  E  D  C  T  G  O  X  Y  C  M  T  F  Z
Y  S  S  R  N  R  L  V  I  Y  W  G  K  N  L  Z
```

1. pig _____

2. on the _____ hand

3. ____ mouth

4. _____ cat

5. _____ sheep

6. night ____

7. ____ eye to eye

8. play it by ____

9. work like a ____

10. someone who is scared

11. pain in the _____

12. sweet _____

13. on the ____ hand

14. _____ turkey

15. too curious about others

16. _____ bird

What is the Idiom?

What is the Idiom?

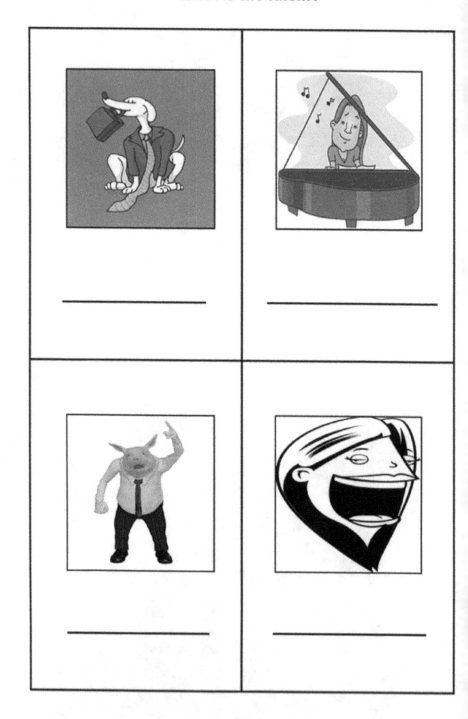

What is the Idiom?

What is the Idiom?

_____   _____

_____   _____

Lesson 3 – Feeling Idioms

Dialogue

Nick: Amy, why the **long face**?
Amy: Well, I have **mixed feelings** about this new job offer. On the one hand, the pay is good. On the other hand, the hours are very long.

Nick: Okay, don't **freak out** about it. Take some time and really decide if it is right for you.
Amy: I just hate not knowing what to do. What if I take the job, and I end up hating it?

Nick: Don't make yourself a **nervous wreck**. I have a feeling you are going to like it.
Amy: I hope you're right. One thing I know for sure is that I'm **sick and tired** of the job I have now.

Nick: Well, **take it easy** and **look on the bright side**. I am taking you out to dinner tonight so that should **cheer you up**.

Definitions:

1. **(a or the) long face** – a sad expression on someone's face. Ex. Why the long face? I just got fired.

2. **(to have) mixed feelings** – to have positive and negative feelings about something or someone. Ex. I have mixed feelings about this job. The money is good, but the hours are long.

3. **(to) freak out** – to have strong fear, anger, or excitement. Ex. She freaked out when I told her a hurricane was coming.

4. **(a) nervous wreck** – a person who feels very nervous. Ex. Tom is a nervous wreck about flying.

5. **(to be) sick and tired** – to not want something anymore. Ex. I am so sick and tired of this company and their crazy rules.

6. **(to) take it easy** – to relax and not worry. Ex. Just take it easy. You will find a job soon.

7. **(to) cheer someone up** – to make someone happy. Ex. A nice long vacation should cheer you up.

8. **(to) look on the bright side** – look at the positive things in a situation. Ex. Even though you have to work on Saturday, look on the bright side. You will get paid overtime.

(a or the) long	(a) nervous wreck	(to) cheer someone up
(to have) mixed feelings	(to be) sick and tired	(to) take it easy
(to) freak out	(to) look on the bright side	

Guess the meaning from the words in the box.

1. _____to have great fear, anger or excitement.

2. _____to have positive and negative feelings about something.

3. _____to be very worried.

4. _____look at a situation in a positive way.

5. _____a sad face.

6. _____to relax and not worry about something.

7. _____to make someone happy.

8. _____to have had enough of something or someone.

Find and correct the one error in each idiom.

1. Take in easy. He will call you soon.

2. Jane said she was sick and tire of waiting for her boyfriend to call her.

3. Steve was a nervous wrench when he took his driving test.

4. We all had mix feelings when Paul left to move to Paris.

5. Please don't freak up about the cost of the tickets.

6. Don't look so sad. I have some news that will cheer you on. We're going to the movies in one hour.

7. Why did he have a long mouth?

8. Look at the bright side. Your car broke down, but you met a handsome mechanic.

long face

mixed feelings

freak out

nervous wreck

sick and tired

take it easy

cheer someone up

look on the bright side

Lesson 4 – Work Idioms

Dialogue

Ben: Harry, you worked all night?
Harry: Yes.

Ben: Wow, you work like a dog! Are they paying you extra?
Harry: No, I just need to finish this project I'm working on.

Ben: Well, I'm worried that I might be **out of work** soon. Steve, in accounting, **stabbed me in the back**. He told the boss that I had another part time job and that I was taking money **under the table**. I'm just trying to **make a living!**
Harry: I wouldn't worry about it. The boss likes you because you are a **jack of all trades**. It's hard to find workers like you that can do anything.

Ben: Maybe you're right.
Harry: If you're still worried about your job being **on the line**, I'll talk to the boss on Monday and remind him what a great worker you are.

Ben: Thanks. That should **do the trick**. I just got **my foot in the door**. I don't want to lose this job.

Definitions:

1. **(to be) out of work** – to be unemployed. Ex. Henry is out of work now.

2. **(to) stab someone in the back** – to betray someone. Ex. Mary stabbed me in the back. She told my boss I was late again.

3. **under the table** – in secret; without being reported. Ex. Some waiters get paid under the table, so they usually have cash.

4. **(to) make a living** – to earn enough money to survive. Ex. How do you make a living? I make a living by driving a taxi.

5. **(a) jack of all trades** - a person who has many skills in different areas. Ex. My uncle is a jack of all trades. He can fix anything: cars, computers, and even phones.

6. **(to be) on the line** - in danger of losing something (usually your job or reputation). Ex. I'm worried my job is on the line. My boss told me he wants to see me in his office this afternoon.

7. **(to) do the trick** – to achieve the result you want. Ex. I can't get that screw to loosen. That big screwdriver should do the trick.

8. **(to get a) foot in the door** – to have an opportunity to start working for a company. Ex. I finally got my foot in the door of a great company.

(to be) out of work   (to) make a living   (to) do the trick

under the table   (a) jack of all trades   on the line

(to get a) foot in the door   (to) stab someone in the back

Guess the meaning from the words in the box.

1. _____someone who can do a little bit of everything.

2. _____at risk or in danger of losing something.

3. _____to get paid in cash (without paying taxes).

4. _____to begin work at a company with a low level job but with a chance of later progress.

5. _____to betray (turn against) someone.

6. _____to be unemployed.

7. _____to earn enough money to survive.

8. _____to succeed; to achieve a desired result.

Find and correct the one error in each idiom.

1. Mark is out a work right now.

2. My old boss stabbed me on the back.

3. Sheila just got her feet in the door of a great advertising company.

4. Matt is a jack of all trade. He has many different skills.

5. When I spoke to Tom yesterday, he said his job was on a line.

6. He makes a leaving driving a taxi.

7. She works as a waitress and makes money under the tables.

8. The doctor said that if I take some aspirin, that should do the tricks.

out of work

stab someone in the back

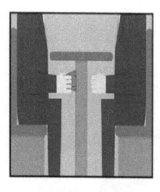

under the table

make a living

jack of all trades

on the line

do the trick

foot in the door

Games for Reviewing

Word Search for Chapters 3 & 4

Read the clues below (1-16) and find the missing part of the idiom or the meaning.

```
V E N J L K B K L O W D L D B H
P C F R O H S M I X E D I H L Q
A L I Z N P A F M J X Y L C Q B
S J Q M G L I N E P J I E J X K
Z S X B D F F K Z S U X H S A N
G T C A J B Z N L F H Z G S S F
C A O U T R Q R Q F O T I R E D
H B M Z H I L F P F O O R C F Q
O F C K I G O D I I D G T I B N
T E S X U H U J J L Z L A D K N
A P A X P T T X A E L V M K I D
B T W S Z F O T C A I D Y U M Q
L C R R Y R Q O K P V J A L L X
E Y U I E Y K H B M I F S Y R G
H U P S C C M A W B N P M C A W
S U O B S K K I H N G S N X C D
```

1. _____ someone in the back

2. a _____ face

3. _____ of all trades

4. _____ in the door

5. on the _____

6. freak ___

7. _____ feelings

8. take it _____

9. under the _____

10. look on the _____ side

11. make a _____

12. nervous _____

13. cheer someone ___

14. sick and _____

15. do the _____

16. ___ of work

What is the Idiom?

What is the Idiom?

What is the Idiom?

What is the Idiom?

_____

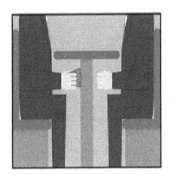

_____

_____

_____

Lesson 5 – Food Idioms

Dialogue

Amanda: Hi, Suzie. Guess what? I met this wonderful man named Jack. He likes to **wine and dine** me.
Suzie: Let's grab a **cup of joe** and talk about it.

Amanda: Okay, but I have to get back to work soon, so I'll make this short. **In a nutshell**, we met online. I was **fed up** with the men I was meeting, so I decided to try something new.
Suzie: Wow! That sounds like it was a **piece of cake** to find him.

Amanda: Well, there were some **fishy** ads, but I stayed away from the **bad apples** and fortunately, I found Jack. Jack is a **big cheese** at his job.
Suzie: I'm so happy for you! Now, let's eat.

Definitions:

1. **(to) wine and dine** – to treat someone to a fancy dinner. Ex. My boyfriend likes to wine and dine me. It's great!

2. **(a) cup of joe** – a cup of coffee. Ex. Let's get a cup of joe.

3. **in a nutshell** – in a few words. It's a long story, but in a nutshell, I got married yesterday.

4. **(to be) fed up** – to feel annoyed or upset about something or someone. Ex. I am so fed up with having to pay so many bills.

5. **(a) piece of cake** – something that is easy. Ex. Learning this job was a piece of cake.

6. **(to be) fishy** – something that causes doubt or distrust. Ex. I don't know. Something is fishy about that man on the train.

7. **(a) bad apple** - a bad person in a group; a bad influence. Ex. Stay away from Michael. He is a bad apple. I saw him fighting yesterday with another kid.

8. **(a *or* the) big cheese** – an important person (usually the boss). Ex. Sam is the big cheese at work. Everyone wants his job.

(to) wine and dine	fed up	(a) bad app
(a) cup of joe	(a) piece of cake	(a or the) big chee:
in a nutshell	fishy	

Guess the meaning from the words in the box.

1. _____in the fewest possible words.

2. _____something really easy.

3. _____not wanting to do something anymore; unable to tolerate.

4. _____a cup of coffee.

5. _____to take someone to an expensive restaurant and pay for their food and drinks.

6. _____causing doubt; suspicious.

7. _____someone who gets into trouble.

8. _____an important person.

Find and correct the one error in each idiom.

1. My mother said my boyfriend was a bad plum because he never went to school.

2. Jane was wined and fed by her husband when they first met.

3. The letter I received seemed fish. It said that I had won $1,000,000.

4. My brother was feed up with politics and said he did not want to vote this year.

5. Math was always a peace of cake for Max.

6. To summarize my plan, here it is in a nut.

7. My friend stopped at the café and bought me a glass of joe.

8. Tom is a big cheesy at work.

wine and dine

cup of joe

in a nutshell

fed up

piece of cake

fishy

bad apple

big cheese

Lesson 6 – Money Idioms

Dialogue

Henry: My father said his friend, Jeff, is rich.
John: Really? What does he do?

Henry: Well, I think he works as an engineer.
John: I wish I was **made of money** like that.

Henry: I know it's hard to **make ends meet** sometimes.
John: I agree. **Time is money** and you have to work hard sometimes and pay **your dues.**

Henry: Well, lunch is **on the house** today.
John: Thanks, Henry, but that's not necessary. We can **go Dutch.**

Henry: You don't need to **shell out** your money this time. I am **paying you back** because last time you paid for me.

Definitions:

1. **(to be) made of money** – to be rich. Ex. My kids think I am made of money. They ask me for money every night!

2. **(to) make ends meet** – to make enough money to live without getting into debt. Ex. It is hard to make ends meet with only a part time job.

3. **time is money** – time is valuable so don't waste it. Ex. Get to work. Time is money.

4. **(to) pay your dues** – to work hard to become successful or be promoted. Ex. It is important to pay your dues if you want success.

5. **(to be) on the house** – it means that your food or drink will be free (the restaurant/bar will not charge you). Ex. Tonight, your meal is on the house since you had to wait two hours.

6. **(to) go Dutch** – to share the cost of something (usually a meal). Ex. Let's go Dutch today. I don't have enough money for both of us.

7. **(to) shell out** – to pay money for something, especially when the cost is unexpected or excessive. Ex. I had to shell out $1500 to fix my car.

8. **(to) pay (someone) back** – to repay money that was borrowed. Ex. I will pay you back tomorrow.

made of money	(to) pay your dues	(to) shell o
(to) make ends meet	on the house	(to) go Dut
time is money	(to) pay someone back	

Guess the meaning from the words in the box.

1. _____to have enough money to pay your bills.

2. _____to share the cost of something.

3. _____someone who is rich.

4. _____free (drinks or food).

5. _____time is valuable, so don't waste it.

6. _____to pay more money than you want to for something.

7. _____to return money that you borrowed from someone.

8. _____to work hard to become successful.

Find and correct the one error in each idiom.

1. If you really want to be the supervisor, you need to pay some dues.

2. My father used to always say, "Time is dollars."

3. Martha works two jobs to make hands meet.

4. The billionaire is make of money.

5. The customer at the bar yelled, "Drinks are on my house."

6. My friend and I always are Dutch when we eat at restaurants.

7. When I loaned my brother money, he said he would definitely pay me bank .

8. I have to shell up money every time I go to the dentist.

made of money

make ends meet

time is money

pay your dues

on the house

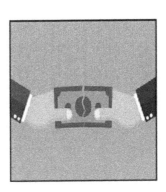

go Dutch

shell out

pay someone back

Games for Reviewing

Word Search for Chapters 5 & 6

Read the clues below (1-16) and find the missing part of the idiom or the meaning.

```
Y  T  M  G  Y  T  C  C  J  C  V  A  U  P  V  N
Q  X  L  O  U  P  E  T  O  M  H  D  S  Y  X  U
M  V  M  H  B  D  V  O  J  G  Y  E  J  W  Q  T
E  K  P  R  R  A  C  M  L  C  O  K  E  Z  T  S
E  J  C  O  J  C  D  B  N  W  I  D  Z  S  T  H
T  I  W  O  E  B  I  N  Q  S  S  P  X  A  E  E
I  V  D  D  C  V  D  E  I  W  P  Q  A  V  Y  L
T  Q  X  E  V  R  I  G  C  N  F  Z  O  Y  S  L
C  R  O  R  P  D  N  G  U  T  L  D  W  G  K  E
X  I  X  O  I  U  E  B  G  O  N  P  W  G  Y  V
M  E  R  O  E  T  X  T  B  F  I  S  H  Y  A  I
M  A  I  G  C  C  C  I  R  L  M  A  K  O  Y  H
O  A  D  Q  E  H  O  M  P  C  O  W  T  Q  Y  M
P  S  X  E  B  R  A  E  G  X  J  E  O  D  K  W
V  T  B  M  S  H  E  L  L  D  U  E  S  Z  X  B
J  O  E  Z  D  G  V  V  H  G  U  M  Q  V  U  J
```

1. in a _____

2. pay your _____

3. fed ___

4. big _____

5. _____ of money

6. cup of ____

7. make ends _____

8. _____ apple

9. _____ someone back

10. go _____

11. _____ is money

12. ___ the house

13. suspicious, doubtful

14. wine and _____

15. _____ of cake

16. _____ out

What is the Idiom?

What is the Idiom?

What is the Idiom?

What is the Idiom?

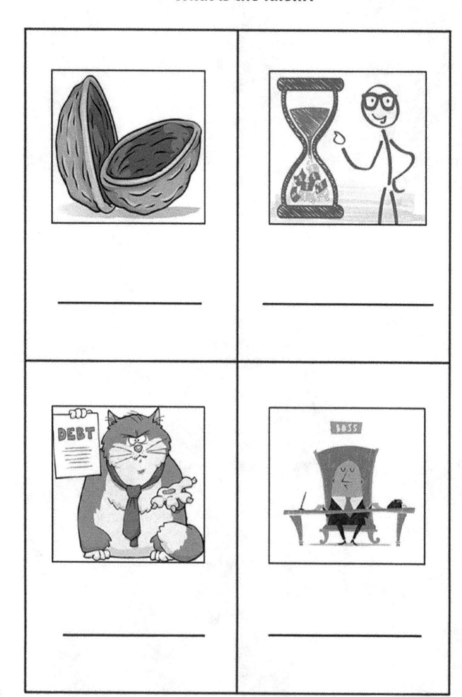

Lesson 7 – People Idioms

Dialogue

Sam: Did I show you this picture of the people on my soccer team?
Tina: No, who's this?

Sam: That's Bob. He's a **hotshot** and very annoying. The guy next to him is Peter, who is a **wise guy**. The coach tries to explain things to him, but he knows it all.
Tina: What about Ed? Didn't you say he was a **couch potato?**

Sam: Yeah, that's right.
Tina: How can he be lazy if he's on your team?

Sam: Well, when he's not playing, he spends all his time relaxing in front of the television. And he's also a **worrywart**. He is constantly worried that our team is going to lose.
Tina: Who is this guy?

Sam: That's Greg. He's a **goody-goody**. He's always trying to be nice to the coach. But most of the time he's just **wishy-washy**.
I asked him to bring some hot dogs to our next meeting. First, he said yes, and then he changed his mind and said he couldn't come to the meeting after all.

Tina: Maybe, he was just being a **cheapskate**.
Sam: Maybe. And that player is me. I'm showing the others how to play.
Tina: Just like when you drive. A typical **backseat driver**.

Definitions:

1. (a) **hotshot** –a person who is talented but too proud of their skills. Ex. My brother is a hotshot lawyer. Every time the family gets together, he tells them how successful he is.

2. (a) **wise guy** – a person who acts as if he knows everything and makes sarcastic comments. Ex. My teenage son is a real wise guy. I asked him how his job was and he said, "I pretend to work, and they pretend to pay me."

3. (a) **couch potato** – a person who spends a lot of time watching television and very little time exercising. Ex. Her husband, Max, is a couch potato. Every night as soon as he gets home from work, he puts the television on, sits on the couch, and stays there all night.

4. (a) **worrywart** – a person who worries about everything. Ex. I try not to be a worry wart, but I worry about every new sickness.

5. (a) **goody-goody** – a person who follows the rules and likes to please people in authority. Ex. I don't think she will come with us to the party. She is a goody-goody.

6. **wishy-washy** –unable to make a decision; weak-willed. Ex. Cindy is wishy-washy. She can never give me a definite answer.

7. (a) **cheapskate** – a person who doesn't like to spend their money; a stingy person. Ex. My date was a real cheapskate. He wanted to take me to eat at a fast food restaurant.

8. (a) **backseat driver** – a person who likes to give orders to other people especially while driving. Ex. Please stop being a backseat driver. I know how to get there.

(a) hotshot	(a) worrywart	(a) cheapska
(a) wise guy	(a) goody-goody	(a) backseat driv
(a) couch potato	wishy-washy	

Guess the meaning from the words in the box.

1. _____ someone who likes to boss other people especially while driving.

2. _____ someone who likes to relax a lot in front of the television and rarely exercises.

3. _____ someone who worries about everything.

4. _____ someone who always does everything right and tries to please people in authority.

5. _____ someone who is talented and lets everyone around him know that.

6. _____ someone who thinks he has all the answers and knows it all.

7. _____ unable to decide.

8. _____ someone who doesn't like to spend money on anything.

Find and correct the one error in each idiom.

1. Her teenage son is a wise boy. He thinks he knows everything.

2. My uncle Tom is a couch tomato.

3. Stop being so washy-wishy. Make a decision!

4. They only had one date because she said he was a cheapkite.

5. My older sister was always a good-good in school.

6. I'm trying to drive. Don't be a backseat drive.

7. Peter's son is a worryguy.

8. That basketball player is a hotshoot.

hotshot

wise guy

couch potato

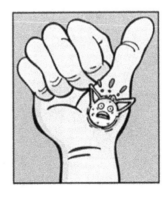

worrywart

goody-goody

wishy-washy

cheapskate

backseat driver

Lesson 8 – Time Idioms

Dialogue

Mother: We have to get up **bright and early** because our plane leaves at 7:00 a.m. So, I think we should wake up around 5:30 a.m., Bobby.
Son: Wow! That's early! I was hoping I could **take my time** getting ready in the morning.

Mother: No, there won't be any time to **dilly-dally** in the morning. You'll have to **shake a leg**.
Son: Mom, it's not fair. Then we get to the airport, and we have to **kill time** waiting for the plane.

Mother: I know, sweetie. You are almost 18 years old, so **in no time**, you will be planning your own trips, and you can choose later flights.
Son: Yeah, I hope **time flies** quickly. I can't wait to get my own place, make my own decisions, and plan my own trips.

Mother: Okay, but **for the time being**, get some sleep.

Definitions:

1. **bright and early** – early in the morning. Ex. She gets up bright and early at 6:00 a.m. to start her day.

2. **(to) take (my) time** – to not want to rush. Ex. Please take your time. We have several hours.

3. **(to) dilly-dally** – to waste time by moving slowly. Ex. Don't dilly dally. We will be late! Turn the television off!

4. **(to) shake a leg** – to hurry up. Ex. Shake a leg. Our plane leaves soon.

5. **(to) kill time** – to waste time waiting for something to happen. Ex. She likes to kill time checking her email.

6. **in no time** – very soon. Ex. Summer will be here in no time.

7. **time flies** – time goes very quickly. Ex. Time flies when you are having fun.

8. **for the time being** – just for now; temporarily. Ex. The plane can't leave yet. For the time being, just relax.

bright and early	(to) shake a leg	time flies
(to) take my time	(to) kill time	in no time
(to) dilly-dally	for the time being	

Guess the meaning from the words in the box.

1. _____hurry up.

2. _____to waste time waiting for something else.

3. _____for now; temporarily.

4. _____to waste time moving slowly.

5. _____very soon.

6. _____very early in the morning.

7. _____time goes very quickly.

8. _____not to rush.

Find and correct the one error in each idiom.

1. Earth flies when you are having fun.

2. In go time, we will be arriving at the airport.

3. Diana needs to get up bright not early, so she can be on time for her new job.

4. When I get up in the morning, I like to get my time to relax.

5. Peter, don't dally-dilly! We need to get to your appointment by 4:00.

6. For the moment being, you should stay in school.

7. Mom, shake your leg! We are going to miss the movie!

8. I often destroy time by checking my email messages on my phone.

bright and early

take my time

dilly-dally

shake a leg

kill time

in no time

time flies

for the time being

Games for Reviewing

Word Search for Chapters 7 & 8

Read the clues below (1-16) and find the missing part of the idiom or the meaning.

```
H E S S H A K E H K X A B I M X O
W T H L B W G D C X A Z R B O P P
Q S O K A V E T I B A H I Z S Z O
F L T Y C U S X K L K I G E M V T
S Q S F K F F F N N L P H A R X B
H Z H M S I G J R O R Y T W M X E
E W O O E Z C A V D D O P P M K I
J S T K A N D U A I J W K N V G N
M J R M T I V L O M P M Y W I Z G
Y O D F H Y V C H E A P S K A T E
W R K V L F G O O D Y Y L W G O W
N H T W H I F W O R R Y L C S D X
E J E I T W E P O T A T O V K B F
U L F A M H A S D F W K K N K X B
R U J Y J E N S N W I Z B B I H Z
J U W Z M C A O H D S U N Q L I N
S J J X F D B E I Y E C X L L X K
```

1. a talented person that brags

2. couch _____

3. for the time _____

4. in ___ time

5. _____wart

6. _____-goody

7. take my ____

8. ____ time

9. _____ guy

10. _____ a leg

11. _____ and early

12. _____ dally

13. time _____

14. a cheap person

15. _____ driver

16. wishy _____

What is the Idiom?

What is the Idiom?

What is the Idiom?

_____   _____

_____   _____

What is the Idiom?

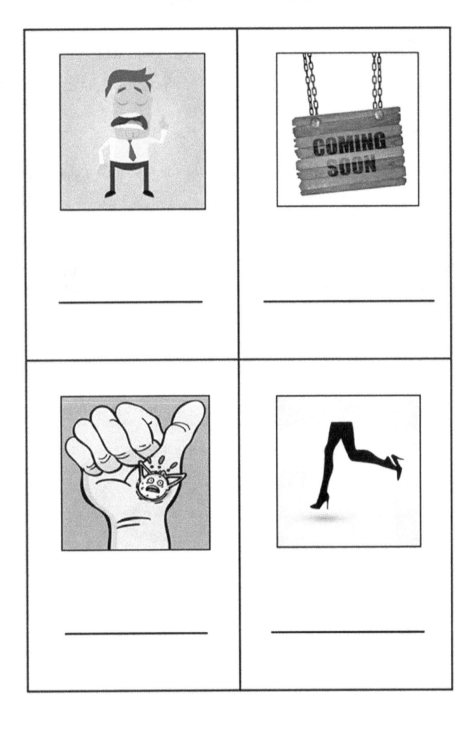

_____   _____

_____   _____

Lesson 9 – Love Idioms

Dialogue

Grandma: How are you, dear?

Sarah: Great, grandma! I have so much to tell you. I went on a **blind date** and met Tony.

Grandma: It sounds like you are **head over heels** in love.

Sarah: I am – we are! So, first, we started **seeing each other** and even **double dated** with two of his friends. It didn't take long for me to **fall in love** with him. Then, shortly after that, he **popped the question.**

Grandma: Wow, that was quick. Do you think you are really ready to **get hitched**?

Sarah: Yes, grandma. I've never been happier. I'm ready to settle down.

Grandma: Well, I would like to meet this young man.

Sarah: You will, grandma, at the wedding.

Definitions:

1. **(a) blind date** – a date with someone you have never seen. Ex. On Tuesday, I will go on a blind date with my cousin's friend, Jim.

2. **head over heels** – to feel very much in love with someone. Ex. I was head over heels about her. I couldn't stop thinking about her.

3. **(to be) seeing someone** – to date one person regularly. Ex. We are seeing each other now. When did you start seeing Frank?

4. **(a) double date** – two couples on a date. Ex. Do you want to go on a double date? Mary and I would like to go out with you and your girlfriend.

5. **(to) fall in love** – to start loving someone romantically. Ex. She always falls in love in the spring.

6. **(to) pop the question** – to ask someone if they want to get married (to propose). Ex. Are you ever going to pop the question? You should ask her tonight.

7. **(to) get hitched** – to get married. Ex. They got hitched last weekend in Las Vegas.

8. **(to) settle down** – to get married and start a family. Ex. I hope he settles down soon with Sheila. She wants a husband and children.

(a) blind date	(a) double date	(to) get hitche
head over heels	(to) fall in love	(to) settle dow
seeing each other	(to) pop the question	

Guess the meaning from the words in the box.

1. _____to get married.

2. _____two couples that go on a date together.

3. _____to propose marriage.

4. _____to be dating someone regularly.

5. _____a date with someone you have never met or seen.

6. _____to start loving someone.

7. _____ to get married and start a family.

8. _____to not be able to stop thinking about someone.

Find and correct the one error in each idiom.

1. Last week, my boyfriend and I went on a trouble date with Mary and Ken.

2. They met at college and fell on love.

3. He asked the question at an expensive restaurant.

4. They were head under heels for each other.

5. Have you ever been on a bind date?

6. They moved to California and decided to settle on.

7. We started seaing each other every night.

8. Tom got pitched last week to Maria.

blind date

head over heels

fall in love

get hitched

seeing each other

settle down

pop the question

double date

Lesson 10 – Funny Idioms

Dialogue

Cindy: Mary, do you want to go to the mall?
Mary: Well, I don't have money right now, but we can go **window shopping**.

Cindy: That's good. Listen, did you know that Kathy has a **sugar daddy?**
Mary: Yeah, I did. But, I thought it was **hush-hush.**

Cindy: I did too. I guess a lot of people know, though.
Mary: She has always been one **tough cookie,** so I'm surprised she feels she wants a man to support her.

Cindy: Well, she acts **as cool as a cucumber** about their relationship.
Mary: True.

Cindy: Last week, I felt like I was going to **kick the bucket.**
Mary: Why?

Cindy: I couldn't stop coughing and when I spoke, it sounded like I had a **frog in my throat.** My coworkers were making fun of me.
Mary: Well, you can't die from a sore throat. You're so dramatic!

Cindy: Not really. So, how much time do we have to "shop" before you have to get back and **punch the clock?**
Mary: We have about an hour and a half.
Cindy: Great!

Definitions:

1. **(to go) window shopping** – to look at items in a window or store without buying anything. Ex. I love to go window shopping in New York.

2. **(a) sugar daddy** – usually a rich older man who gives gifts or money to a younger woman for her companionship. Ex. Suzie has a sugar daddy who pays all her bills.

3. **hush-hush** – secret. Ex. No one knows yet about the company losing money. It's hush-hush.

4. **(a) tough cookie** – a strong determined person who usually succeeds in difficult situations. Ex. Mary is such a tough cookie. After she got divorced, she raised four children all by herself.

5. **(as) cool as a cucumber** – confident and self-assured. Ex. Only one of the people being interviewed looked as cool as a cucumber.

6. **(to) kick the bucket** – to die. Ex. Before I kick the bucket, I plan to go to Paris.

7. **(to have a) frog in my throat** – to have difficulty speaking because of dryness, a cold, or other respiratory issue. Ex. Sorry. I feel like I have a frog in my throat. My throat really hurts.

8. **(to) punch the clock** – to record on a machine when you start and end work. Ex. I have to punch the clock when I get to work every day.

(to go) window shopping	(a) tough cookie	(to) kick the buck
(a) sugar daddy	hush-hush	(as) cool as a cucumb
(to) punch the clock	(to have a) frog in my throat	

Guess the meaning from the words in the box.

1. _____to put a time card into a machine to show when you start and end work.

2. _____secret.

3. _____cool and confident.

4. _____to die.

5. _____a strong person who has handled many difficulties.

6. _____when you have difficulty speaking because of a cold or other related problem.

7. _____to look at items in store windows but not buy anything.

8. _____usually a rich older man who pays a younger woman's bills, food, etc. to be with her.

Find and correct the one error in each idiom.

1. The beautiful young woman has a sweet daddy to help her.

2. She must be a tough woman to be able to work two jobs and go to school.

3. The company said their plans for the future were hushy-hush.

4. When Jane gets to work, she has to hit the clock.

5. Max is as cool in a cucumber.

6. Before my neighbor kicked a bucket, he said, "Don't worry, be happy."

7. The student sounds like she has a frog in her mouth.

8. Let's go street shopping before the stores close.

kick the bucket

hush-hush

cool as a cucumber

window shopping

sugar daddy

tough cookie

punch the clock

frog in the throat

Games for Reviewing

Word Search for Chapters 9 & 10

Read the clues below (1-16) and find the missing part of the idiom or the meaning.

```
K F E H J R B K I X A W B G B O X
G M C E O I C L Q L L I C C G E T
Z R F E C O O L I V J N K C E R N
P R V L S M Y O Y N V D J O G N O
U E K S Y G L X L V D O I O A W S
W W T H R O A T I X V W L K T Q E
T M P B W I F U X S Y C K I X E T
P G O G Y Y A F Y K W S J E J Q T
D G P T K S L U I A A B E J L B L
M D C R E D L K F H L M G E J V E
X O L Y W F H Q M U I L G F I B U
O U P U N C H J X S S U G A R N Z
C B H K F A V M T H F J U Q G Q G
S L B E T I X W W L K I C K N M J
Y E V H T Z B X C N H G K J W K B
Y P F C D I X W J N J R D U X F N
F T B J P I O G X E Q G J T P Y D
```

1. ____ hitched

2. ____ the question

3. _____ date

4. _____ daddy

5. head over _____

6. _____ as a cucumber

7. _____ shopping

8. _____ in love

9. _____ each other

10. frog in the _____

11. _____ date

12. _____ the clock

13. _____ down

14. _____ the bucket

15. _____-hush

16. tough _____

What is the Idiom?

What is the Idiom?

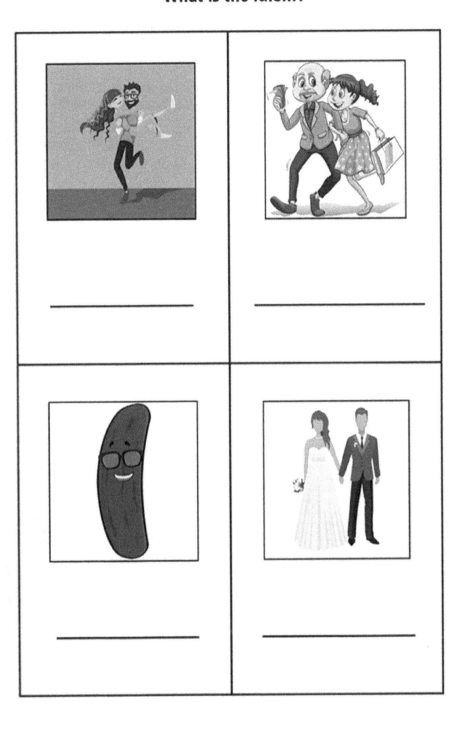

What is the Idiom?

What is the Idiom?

Answers

Guess the Meaning

Pg. 4
1. pigheaded
2. work like a dog
3. black sheep
4. copycat
5. chicken
6. cold turkey
7. early bird
8. night owl

Pg. 10
1. play it by ear
2. on the other hand
3. pain in the neck
4. see eye to eye
5. nosy
6. big mouth
7. on the one hand
8. sweet tooth

Pg. 21
1. freak out
2. mixed feelings
3. nervous wreck
4. look on the bright side
5. long face
6. take it easy
7. cheer someone up
8. sick and tired

Find the Error

Pg. 5
1. chicken
2. pigheaded
3. cold
4. black
5. a (dog)
6. owl
7. copy
8. bird

Pg. 11
1. nosy
2. neck
3. the (not my)
4. hand
5. it (by ear)
6. tooth
7. big
8. to (eye)

Pg. 22
1. it (easy)
2. tired
3. wreck
4. mixed
5. out
6. up
7. face
8. on (the bright side)

Guess the Meaning	Find the Error
Pg. 27	**Pg. 28**
1. jack of all trades	1. of (work)
2. on the line	2. in (the back)
3. under the table	3. foot
4. foot in the door	4. trades
5. stab someone in the back	5. the (line)
6. out of work	6. living
7. make a living	7. table
8. do the trick	8. trick
Pg. 38	**Pg. 39**
1. in a nutshell	1. apple
2. piece of cake	2. dined
3. fed up	3. fishy
4. cup of joe	4. fed
5. wine and dine	5. piece
6. fishy	6. nutshell
7. bad apple	7. cup
8. big cheese	8. cheese
Pg. 44	**Pg. 45**
1. make ends meet	1. your (dues)
2. go Dutch	2. money
3. made of money	3. ends
4. on the house	4. made
5. time is money	5. the (house)
6. shell out	6. go (Dutch)
7. pay someone back	7. back
8. pay your dues	8. out
Pg. 55	**Pg. 56**
1. backseat driver	1. guy
2. couch potato	2. potato

Guess the Meaning

3. worrywart
4. goody-goody
5. hotshot
6. wise guy
7. wishy-washy
8. cheapskate

Pg. 61
1. shake a leg
2. kill time
3. for the time being
4. dilly-dally
5. in no time
6. bright and early
7. time flies
8. take (my) time

Pg. 72
1. get hitched
2. double date
3. pop the question
4. seeing each other
5. blind date
6. fall in love
7. settle down
8. head over heels

Pg. 78
1. punch the clock
2. hush-hush
3. cool as a cucumber
4. kick the bucket
5. tough cookie
6. frog in (my) throat
7. window shopping
8. sugar daddy

Find the Error

3. wishy-washy
4. cheapskate
5. goody-goody
6. driver
7. wart
8. hotshot

Pg. 62
1. Time
2. no
3. and (early)
4. take
5. dilly-dally
6. time
7. a (shake a leg)
8. kill

Pg. 73
1. double
2. in (love)
3. popped
4. over
5. blind
6. down
7. seeing
8. hitched

Pg. 79
1. sugar
2. cookie
3. hush-hush
4. punch
5. as (a cucumber)
6. the (bucket)
7. throat
8. window

Word Search Answers to Puzzles

Word Search for Chapters 1 & 2

Read the clues below (1-16) and find the missing part of the idiom or the meaning.

```
B H F B A S T N Z D B E R B L E
C I J T C M A X W J R D N K W Y
X Y G T O B H A H N E C K K K W
T S A A L W H T X K V H C F E E
B H E U D N O S Y Q E A R L Y L
G I V E F J J K V I B P A L Q C
U C O P Y Y V H X J T O O T H P
F U H E A D E D D K U F A S L O
D B W X F E A R G D J T V E X W
L O K C K R F M W V A G X D X L
A K G X V C H I C K E N O L N C
V O L O E B K Q B Z U M B N C M
B G C T Z W K K K L C W V V E F
Q A B H R S Y O I F A K A N Y R
U D Q E D C T G O X Y C M T F Z
Y S S R N R L V I Y W G K N L Z
```

1. pig_____

2. on the _____hand

3. _____ mouth

4. _____cat

5. _____ sheep

6. night _____

7. _____ eye to eye

8. play it by _____

9. work like a _____

10. someone who is scared

11. pain in the _____

12. sweet _____

13. on the _____ hand

14. _____ turkey

15. too curious about others

16. _____ bird

Word Search for Chapters 3 & 4

Read the clues below (1-16) and find the missing part of the idiom or the meaning.

```
V  E  N  J  L  K  B  K  L  O  W  D  L  D  B  H
P  C  F  R  O  H  S  M  I  X  E  D  I  H  L  Q
A  L  I  Z  N  P  A  F  M  J  X  Y  L  C  Q  B
S  J  Q  M  G  L  I  N  E  P  J  I  E  J  X  K
Z  S  X  B  D  F  F  K  Z  S  U  X  H  S  A  N
G  T  C  A  J  B  Z  N  L  F  H  Z  G  S  S  F
C  A  O  U  T  R  Q  R  Q  F  O  T  I  R  E  D
H  B  M  Z  H  I  L  F  P  F  O  O  R  C  F  Q
O  F  C  K  I  G  O  D  I  I  D  G  T  I  B  N
T  E  S  X  U  H  U  J  J  L  Z  L  A  D  K  N
A  P  A  X  P  T  T  X  A  E  L  V  M  K  I  D
B  T  W  S  Z  F  O  T  C  A  I  D  Y  U  M  Q
L  C  R  R  Y  R  Q  O  K  P  V  J  A  L  L  X
E  Y  U  I  E  Y  K  H  B  M  I  F  S  Y  R  G
H  U  P  S  C  C  M  A  W  B  N  P  M  C  A  W
S  U  O  B  S  K  K  I  H  N  G  S  N  X  C  D
```

1. _____ someone in the back

2. a _____ face

3. _____ of all trades

4. _____ in the door

5. on the _____

6. freak _____

7. _____ feelings

8. take it _____

9. under the _____

10. look on the _____ side

11. make a _____

12. nervous _____

13. cheer someone ___

14. sick and _____

15. do the _____

16. ___ of work

Word Search for Chapters 5 & 6

Read the clues below (1-16) and find the missing part of the idiom or the meaning

```
Y  T  M  G  Y  T  C  C  J  C  V  A  U  P  V  N
Q  X  L  O  U  P  E  T  O  M  H  D  S  Y  X  U
M  V  M  H  B  D  V  O  J  G  Y  E  J  W  Q  T
E  K  P  R  R  A  C  M  L  C  O  K  E  Z  T  S
E  J  C  O  J  C  D  B  N  W  I  D  Z  S  T  H
T  I  W  O  E  B  I  N  Q  S  S  P  X  A  E  E
I  V  D  D  C  V  D  E  I  W  P  Q  A  V  Y  L
T  Q  X  E  V  R  I  G  C  N  F  Z  O  Y  S  L
C  R  O  R  P  D  N  G  U  T  L  D  W  G  K  E
X  I  X  O  I  U  E  B  G  O  N  P  W  G  Y  V
M  E  R  O  E  T  X  T  B  F  I  S  H  Y  A  I
M  A  I  G  C  C  C  I  R  L  M  A  K  O  Y  H
O  A  D  Q  E  H  O  M  P  C  O  W  T  Q  Y  M
P  S  X  E  B  R  A  E  G  X  J  E  O  D  K  W
V  T  B  M  S  H  E  L  L  D  U  E  S  Z  X  B
J  O  E  Z  D  G  V  V  H  G  U  M  Q  V  U  J
```

1. in a _____

2. pay your _____

3. fed _____

4. big _____

5. _____ of money

6. cup of _____

7. make ends _____

8. _____ apple

9. _____ someone back

10. go _____

11. _____ is money

12. _____ the house

13. suspicious, doubtful

14. wine and _____

15. _____ of cake

16. _____ out

Word Search for Chapters 7 & 8

Read the clues below (1-16) and find the missing part of the idiom or the meaning.

```
H  E  S  S  H  A  K  E  H  K  X  A  B  I  M  X  O
W  T  H  L  B  W  G  D  C  X  A  Z  R  B  O  P  P
Q  S  O  K  A  V  E  T  I  B  A  H  I  Z  S  Z  O
F  L  T  Y  C  U  S  X  K  L  K  I  G  E  M  V  T
S  Q  S  F  K  F  F  F  N  N  L  P  H  A  R  X  B
H  Z  H  M  S  I  G  J  R  O  R  Y  T  W  M  X  E
E  W  O  O  E  Z  C  A  V  D  D  O  P  P  M  K  I
J  S  T  K  A  N  D  U  A  I  J  W  K  N  V  G  N
M  J  R  M  T  I  V  L  O  M  P  M  Y  W  I  Z  G
Y  O  D  F  H  Y  V  C  H  E  A  P  S  K  A  T  E
W  R  K  V  L  F  G  O  O  D  Y  Y  L  W  G  O  W
N  H  T  W  H  I  F  W  O  R  R  Y  L  C  S  D  X
E  J  E  I  T  W  E  P  O  T  A  T  O  V  K  B  F
U  L  F  A  M  H  A  S  D  F  W  K  K  N  K  X  B
R  U  J  Y  J  E  N  S  N  W  I  Z  B  B  I  H  Z
J  U  W  Z  M  C  A  O  H  D  S  U  N  Q  L  I  N
S  J  J  X  F  D  B  E  I  Y  E  C  X  L  L  X  K
```

1. a talented person that brags

2. couch _____

3. for the time _____

4. in ___ time

5. _____ wart

6. _____-goody

7. take my ____

8. ____ time

9. _____ guy

10. _____ a leg

11. _____ and early

12. _____ daily

13. time _____

14. a cheap person

15. _____ driver

16. wishy _____

Word Search for Chapters 9 & 10

Read the clues below (1-16) and find the missing part of the idiom or the meaning.

```
K F E H J R B K I X A W B G B O X
G M C E O I C L Q L L I C C G E T
Z R F E C O O L I V J N K C E R N
P R V L S M Y O Y N V D J O G N O
U E K S Y G L X L V D O I O A W S
W W T H R O A T I X V W L K T Q E
T M P B W I F U X S Y C K I X E T
P G O G Y Y A F Y K W S J E J Q T
D G P T K S L U I A A B E J L B L
M D C R E D L K F H L M G E J V E
X O L Y W F H Q M U I L G F I B U
O U P U N C H J X S S U G A R N Z
C B H K F A V M T H F J U Q G Q G
S L B E T I X W W L K I C K N M J
Y E V H T Z B X C N H G K J W K B
Y P F C D I X W J N J R D U X F N
F T B J P I O G X E Q G J T P Y D
```

1. ____ hitched

2. ____ the question

3. _____ date

4. _____ daddy

5. head over _____

6. _____ as a cucumber

7. _____ shopping

8. _____ in love

9. _____ each other

10. frog in the _____

11. _____ date

12. _____ the clock

13. _____ down

14. _____ the bucket

15. _____ -hush

16. tough _____

Answers to What is the Idiom?

Chapters 1 and 2

Pg. 15	
early bird	sweet tooth
nosy	copycat
Pg. 16	
work like a dog	play it by ear
pigheaded	big mouth
Pg. 17	
night owl	on the other hand
chicken	pain in the neck
Pg. 18	
black sheep	on the other hand (or one)
cold turkey	see eye to eye

Chapters 3 and 4

Pg. 32	
freak out	jack of all trades
cheer up	stab someone in the back
Pg. 33	
nervous wreck	take it easy
make a living	out of work
Pg. 34	
foot in the door	long face
mixed feelings	on the line
Pg. 35	
look on the bright side	under the table
sick and tired	do the trick

Chapters 5 and 6

Pg. 49	
piece of cake	go Dutch
shell out	bad apple
Pg. 50	
make ends meet	fishy
made of money	fed up
Pg. 51	
wine and dine	on the house
pay your dues	cup of joe
Pg. 52	
in a nutshell	time is money
pay someone back	big cheese

Chapters 7 and 8

Pg. 66	
backseat driver	kill time
bright and early	hotshot
Pg. 67	
cheapskate	dilly-dally
time flies	goody-goody
Pg. 68	
for the time being	take my time
wishy-washy	couch potato
Pg. 69	
wise guy	in no time
worrywart	shake a leg

Chapters 9 and 10

Pg. 83	
hush-hush	pop the question
settle down	frog in my throat
Pg. 84	
fall in love	sugar daddy
cool as a cucumber	get hitched
Pg. 85	
kick the bucket	double date
tough cookie	blind date
Pg. 86	
seeing each other	punch the clock
window shopping	head over heels

Idiom Glossary

backseat driver - someone who likes to boss others especially while driving

bad apple - a bad person in a group; a bad influence

big cheese - an important person (usually the boss)

big mouth – someone who talks too much or reveals secrets

black sheep - a person who embarrasses a group or family because the person is different or has gotten into trouble

blind date - a date with someone you have never seen

bright and early - early in the morning

cheapskate - someone who doesn't like to spend their money; a cheap person

cheer (someone) up – to make someone happy **chicken** - afraid of something or someone

cold turkey - to quit something completely

cool as a cucumber - confident and self-assured

copycat - someone who copies another person's clothes, ideas, or behavior

couch potato - someone who spends a lot of time watching television and very little time exercising

cup of joe - a cup of coffee

dilly-dally - to waste time by moving slowly

do the trick – achieve the desired result

double date – an evening or outing for two couples on a date

early bird - someone who gets up early or arrives early

fall in love - to start loving someone

fed up - annoyed or upset about something or someone

fishy – suspicious; hard to believe

foot in the door - an opportunity to start at a company and later progress

for the time being - just for now; temporarily

freak out - to have strong fear, anger, or excitement

frog in my throat - to have difficulty speaking because of dryness, a cold, or other respiratory issue

get hitched - to get married

go Dutch - to share the cost of something (usually a meal)

goody-goody - someone who follows the rules and likes to please people in authority

head over heels - to be very much in love with someone

hotshot - someone who is talented but brags about it

hush-hush – secret; private

in a nutshell - to summarize something; in short

in no time - very soon

jack of all trades - a person who has many skills in different areas

kick the bucket - to die

kill time - to waste time waiting for something to happen

long face - to look sad

look on the bright side – to focus on the positive things; to be optimistic.

made of money - rich

make a living - to earn enough money to survive

make ends meet - to make enough money to live on without getting into debt

mixed feelings – to have contradictory feelings

nervous wreck - a very nervous person

night owl - someone who likes to stay up all night

nosy - too interested in finding out information about other people

on the house – free (the restaurant/bar will not charge you)

on the line - in danger of losing something (usually your job or reputation)

on the one hand - as the first of two contrasting ideas

on the other hand - as the second contrasting idea

out of work - unemployed

pain in the neck - a difficult or annoying thing or person

pay (someone) back - to return money that was borrowed

pay your dues - to work hard to become successful

piece of cake - something that's easy

pigheaded - stubborn, not willing to change their mind

play it by ear – to be spontaneous; to act without planning

pop the question - to ask someone if they want to get married (to propose)

punch the clock - to record on a machine when you start and end work

see eye to eye - to agree with someone

seeing someone - to date one person regularly

settle down - to get married and start a family

shake a leg – to hurry up

shell out - to pay money for something, especially when the cost is unexpected and excessive

sick and tired - not wanting something anymore

stab (someone) in the back - betrayed

sugar daddy - usually a rich older man who gives gifts or money to a younger woman for her companionship

sweet tooth – a preference for sweets

take it easy – to relax and not to worry

take (my) time - not to rush

time flies - time goes very quickly

time is money - time is valuable, so don't waste it

tough cookie - a strong person who usually succeeds in difficult situations

under the table - secretly; without being reported

window shopping - looking at items in a window or store without buying anything

wine and dine - to take someone out to a fancy dinner

wise guy - someone who acts as if he knows everything and makes sarcastic comments

wishy-washy - someone unable to make decisions

work like a dog - to work very hard

worrywart - someone who worries about everything

CPSIA information can be obtained
at www.ICGtesting.com
Printed in the USA
FSHW010948250321
79848FS